# What Our Readers Have Said...

**Applicability**

*"These books are great tools that should be used as guidelines for our everyday supervisory practices. You need to take the time to do a short self-evaluation when reading them."*

•

*"The Pinpoint Training Series delivers information that could be used in a lot different areas."*

•

*"The things and problems we deal with everyday are discussed in these books."*

**Convenience**

*"I like this because I can take them with me to read at a convenient time. I feel the little time I have to spend in the office is best use on activities that directly relate to revenue opportunities. I like the short amount of time it takes to keep up with these."*

•

*"I prefer the self-study approach; it fits in with my schedule."*

•

*"I like the fact that the format allows the books to be reviewed as time permits. All work has been conducted on personal, evening/weekend time."*

•

*"Easy to use... if you put the time into it."*

## Challenge

*"My thought is that the real value of these books comes into effect when doing the action plans."*

•

*"I like the fact that the format allows assignments to be reviewed as time permits."*

## Clarity

*"Short and sweet. These books are easy to comprehend."*

•

*"Easy to use, understand, and reference if needed."*

## Relevance

*"I have enjoyed reading these books. They are relevant to today's work environment and the ongoing change in the way we manage our workforce."*

•

*"I believe the contents of the Pinpoint series are excellent. It causes one to reflect on the daily dynamics in working with oneself as well as with management and peers."*

# The Impact of Change on Individuals

*Pinpoint Leadership Skill Development Training Series*

TIMOTHY F. BEDNARZ

MAJORIUM
BUSINESS PRESS

Pinpoint Leadership Skill Development Training Series
*"The Impact of Change on Individuals"*
Timothy F. Bednarz

Graphic design: Monika Pawlak

Majorium Business Press
2025 Main Street
Stevens Point, WI 54481
715.342.1018 • 800.654.4935



ISBN 978-1-882181-75-9

Printed in the United States of America

# Introduction

*The Pinpoint Leadership Skill Development Training Series* is designed for targeted training and education regarding increased improvement in a specific skill or competency.

Each book within this series is designed to be easy to use, understand and apply to your job. It can be used as a basis for training individuals, as a discussion guide or as a personal training tool.

Each chapter within this book discusses a specific concept. When you have completed all eight chapters you should have a 360° perspective of the topic.

Additionally, each chapter is divided into specific sections:

- The first section provides you with an overview of the topic
- The Implications section discusses why the concept is important, and why it is important to learn and apply.
- The Strategies, Tips & Techniques to Apply section teaches how to use and apply the particular concept to your work.
- The Points to Ponder section gives you something to think about or to be discussed with a group setting. These are questions not meant to be immediately answered, but to be pondered over time.
- The Training Activity section provides you with the tools to transfer what you have learned to your job. It is designed to help create an action plan to effectively apply the concept.

Each of the topics in this series is time-tested and proven in the marketplace. They have been used by thousands of employees as training tools. Many of the users have commented that what made these books valuable, was the ability to refer to them when a problem surfaced. They indicated that they remembered reading about the exact problem. They referred back to these books and found an appropriate solution.

You will find them equally valuable as a resource in your professional development library.

# Table of Contents

## LEARNING OBJECTIVES:

- To identify the critical incremental factors and implications of change and their impact on individuals within the workplace.
- To identify and analyze the reasons why change is needed and important.
- To define the personal impacts of change upon individuals within the work environment.
- How to recognize when change is taking place.
- To determine the personal ramifications of change upon individuals.
- How to apply strategies to manage change.
- To identify and determine how decision making is impacted by change and how it needs to be modified and altered accordingly.
- To identify and apply strategies to personally manage change successfully.
- To analyze and apply techniques to prevent personal burnout.

# 1

# The Challenges That Change Presents

Change presents specific and direct challenges to both leaders and groups. For some, the challenge is to initiate change. For others, it's a trial to handle the momentum of change within the organization. Still others find it challenging to ultimately accept and integrate changes made.

Leaders must overcome each of these challenges. They are fundamentally interdependent, and success in handling one may impact how someone deals with the others.

## IMPLICATIONS — WHAT THIS MEANS TO YOU

Like it or not, both leaders and groups must deal with the forces of change that impact their organizations. They will find that stronger change initiatives amount to more difficult challenges. The reason for this correlation is that, for many organizations facing change, a systematic response is set in motion where the maintenance of a balance or the status quo is the natural process. Greater change thus equals greater resistance.

It is important for leaders to understand that the earlier and more clearly they can anticipate challenges, the easier it will be to cope. The ideal time to handle challenges is before they actually occur. Doing so will minimize the time and energy needed to deal with the inevitable problems that later spring from each challenge. In this way, leaders can establish a mindset where they see challenges as steppingstones to successfully implementing change.

## STRATEGIES, TIPS & TECHNIQUES TO APPLY

Whether confronting change individually or in a group setting, leaders will undoubtedly face a series of challenges. These challenges may appear singular, and each can certainly be handled and resolved as an individual issue, but, for best results, leaders must confront these elements as an ensemble of forces that need to be worked on as a whole.

Both leaders and groups will find that these challenges will immediately surface anytime they begin to do something different or conduct themselves in an unfamiliar way. Several of these challenges are discussed below.

### Time

When facing change, leaders and groups may immediately feel pressed for time. Individuals will argue that, with all of the tasks, assignments and initiatives they are responsible for already, they don't have any time for new initiatives. They presume that the implementation of change initiatives diverts scarce resources—the first of which is time—away from existing processes.

### Support

While senior management often mandates change initiatives, they may fail to provide the support that leaders feel they need to carry out a successful implementation. As a result, leaders and groups often think they lack the needed resources, training and guidance to initiate mandates. The key challenge is to develop the internal resources to build capacity for change within the organization.

### Relevance

Many individuals who resist a particular change will argue that it is not relevant to the organization's goals and mission. Leaders and groups are challenged to make a case for change within the organization. They must articulate an appropriate business focus that clearly and distinctly demonstrates that their efforts are relevant and support the organization's goals.

### Consistency

Change is not instantaneous, nor can it be turned on and off like a light switch. Rather, it is an incremental process. The problem is that resisters of change will often exclaim that the words and actions of leaders and groups—or anyone who is championing change in the organization—are inconsistent with the values they are espousing.

### Anxiety

Leaders and groups who deal with change or implement change initiatives can be challenged by their own fears and anxieties that are triggered by concerns over personal exposure, vulnerability and inadequacy. These fears can also be ignited by the conflict caused by increasing levels of candor and openness as well as low levels of trust within the organization.

### Assessment

Leaders and groups will face the prospect of receiving a negative assessment of their performance by opponents of change within the organization. Their evaluation will be based on traditional ways of measuring success, such as metrics and time horizons.

### Isolation

As leaders and group members develop into true believers of change, they will be challenged by both isolation and arrogance. They may feel they have developed the right way to do things and that nonbelievers within the organization don't understand them. This results in miscommunication, misinterpretation and, ultimately, isolation and arrogance.

## Control and Governance

As leaders and groups seek greater autonomy in implementing change, they may face the challenge of managers trying to exert preventative controls. Such managers will be concerned about additional autonomy potentially leading to chaos and internal fragmentation. It can simply be a power struggle over control, with the manager feeling threatened by changes.

## Diffusion

Many leaders and groups will find it challenging to diffuse their knowledge across organizational boundaries. The resulting difficulty is that other leaders and groups traveling down similar paths may not be able to build upon already achieved successes; therefore, they end up wasting resources while essentially "reinventing the wheel."

## Purpose

Leaders and groups are challenged to revitalize and change the "thinking" of the organization. By ushering in and harnessing the positive impact of change, leaders and groups will shift the company's focus and identity.

### POINTS TO PONDER – SOMETHING TO THINK ABOUT

1. Were you aware of the challenges that you have to overcome as a leader?
2. What personal capabilities can you utilize to overcome these challenges?

## TRAINING ACTIVITY — APPLICATION & ACTION PLAN

Identify challenges you must personally overcome.

1. Determine which forces might counter your efforts.
2. Attempt to understand the nature of the challenges before you.
    a. What is your perspective?
    b. Try to can change your perspective and see the situation differently.

# 2

# The Process of Change

The power of change begins with the personal commitment and passion of a single individual who partners with a small number of devoted people. Success depends upon this core of people who share each other's values and passions.

## IMPLICATIONS — WHAT THIS MEANS TO YOU

The process of change is a deeply personal experience for leaders. Without their personal conviction, passion and dedication, they would not have the power or desire to move forward. Thus, leaders must change internally before they have the capability of implementing change in their organization.

If leaders examined the great movements and societies throughout history, they would discover a common factor: the power and conviction of a single person surrounded by a small group of committed followers. While change often originates with one person, dedicated group partnerships magnify that power and produce a potent force for change.

## STRATEGIES, TIPS & TECHNIQUES TO APPLY

There are three fundamental interrelated forces required to sustain profound change in any organization. Leaders utilize these forces to bridge internal differences and overcome organizational problems and barriers resistant to change. These forces are discussed in more detail below.

## Personal Results

First and foremost, a change must occur within the individual leader. While individuals are motivated and have a passion to produce results, those results often are not business or organizational, but related to the quality of their personal lives.

Research has demonstrated that individuals who discover a direct personal benefit in doing something will then find the initial source of energy and passion to sustain profound change. That is, personal results are always important, whether at work or home, whether leader or subordinate. Individuals are satisfied with their jobs when they work with other people they can trust and with whom they share a sense of purpose. When it comes to supporting change initiatives in the workplace, an individual's enthusiasm and willingness to commit increases when he or she realizes personal results and benefits.

## Networks of Committed People

When the mode of participation is changed, then the organization as a whole is changed. Research on the nature of change and innovation in an organization has consistently pointed to the importance of informal networks of people. These networks are vital for individuals to learn about new ideas, to support and coach one another and to share practical knowledge and expertise. When these networks operate in an organization, employees rely upon one another to get their work done. They are bound by a common sense of purpose and a real need to share knowledge and expertise. These are the critical building blocks for organizational change.

As more people participating in change initiatives become part of extended networks, information spreads more quickly and widely, creating interest in and the impetus for additional change.

## Business Results

The impact of personal commitment and the formation of informal networks of people produce changes in business practices. Often, the first thing to happen is an elimination of wasteful processes ingrained in the organization. Over time, new and more effective practices are invented and implemented that increase results. As these new procedures lead to better results, the credibility of change to produce positive outcomes increases in the organization. Seeing these results, employees begin to feel that change involves less personal risk. Resistance to change is thus reduced and individuals become more willing to commit themselves to initiatives. Personal benefits from change increase, which helps renew the entire cycle and advance the organization.

## Integration

As the three aforementioned forces come into practice, they operate simultaneously. The result is a distinct set of forces capable of sustaining change and growth. Additionally, the forces are interdependent: a positive change in one can strengthen the others, which serves to increase the power and velocity of the entire cycle.

### POINTS TO PONDER – SOMETHING TO THINK ABOUT

1. How has a personal commitment of yours impacted your ability to lead and perform on the job?
2. Have you developed a personal passion for your work?

### TRAINING ACTIVITY – APPLICATION & ACTION PLAN

Since change begins with one individual, analyze your personal motivation.

1. Identify the personal benefits you derive from your work related to:
    a. Your passions
    b. Your ideas
2. Set boundaries that allow you to make healthy life choices that keep you balanced.

# 3

# How Change Personally Impacts Leaders

Change is a reality that has caused the business environment to undergo structural changes. Decisions are made faster, technology continues to fuel change and the sense of stability once experienced by many businesses has evaporated. As change continues to occur, it impacts leaders and forces them to make critical choices to deal with change in their company.

## IMPLICATIONS – WHAT THIS MEANS TO YOU

Most companies have grown and become more efficient at what they do. This model was established at the dawn of the Industrial Age and has been followed through the years by many successful companies; it prescribed that companies reduce risk, increase reliability, reduce variability and increase efficiency. However, at the dawn of the Information Age, change began to affect businesses with increased speed and greater dynamics, subsequently altering the once firmly established business model. Many people have learned that what once worked in the past, often can lead to an organization's demise.

Leaders must understand that change and everything associated with it is here to stay. How they react and adapt to change is of the utmost importance. When leaders accept the realities of change and lead their organizations through a continual series of steps, they remove the obstructions to adaptation and take advantage of the momentum that change can bring. The leader that resists change ends up focusing his or her energies on tasks that are self-defeating and counterproductive.

## STRATEGIES, TIPS & TECHNIQUES TO APPLY

Change and all of its ramifications affect all leaders, managers and employees, no matter what. The company's collective posture and attitude determines the impact that change will have upon their business. What follows is a discussion of the typical attitudes (some negative, some positive) that managers and leaders will have when faced with change.

### Fear

Nobody likes change. It threatens the comfort zone that all individuals and organizations have created. People see change as something fearful that can jeopardize their survival, job and organization. For such individuals, the daily changes that confront them during every interaction are viewed not as opportunities, but threats.

Powerful individuals in an organization are especially threatened by change. As they see it, what they have worked hard for all of their lives is now in danger; their reality and goals in life have been challenged. Most hope that changes are temporary and will suddenly go away. Rather than manage change, change begins to manage them.

### Ignorance

When individuals fear change, they have a natural tendency to ignore it, hoping that the situation will revert back to the way it once was. In reality, their resistance to change leads to a professional demise that either happens quickly or lingers on painfully. Most individuals understand a quick ruin, but ignore the lingering kind. Even though the end results are the same, when the situation drags on they always hold on to the hope that things might clear up and that their end will never come.

Leaders who fear the immediate impact of change worry that the organization may downsize, that their jobs will be lost or that facilities will be closed. Change may produce these same consequences down the road as well, with the experience being prolonged and painful. In such a case, the organization will be destabilized by the long-term impact of change, and many leaders will ignore it, continuing to simply hope for the best.

### Resistance

After the initial stages of ignorance, many managers will actively resist change within their organizations. Their fears will turn into anger and hostility as they fail to realize, like it or not, the forces of change will ultimately win. They don't understand that change is the "new normal." While the workplace once experienced a series of stable moments interrupted by episodes of change, it is now transformed into an environment of nearly continuous change with occasional moments of stability. Leaders who resist these alterations fail to comprehend that change will always defeat them unless they learn to work with it.

### Acceptance

More astute leaders understand that they cannot defeat change and that it ultimately offers them new opportunities to innovate, become more productive and enter into and capture new markets. These leaders realize they can use the force and impetus of change to create positive momentum and outcomes. They comprehend, furthermore, that the power of change can be harnessed to drive their organization forward. For all this to occur, the dynamics of the organization must be redefined to take advantage of new opportunities.

### Evolution

The enlightened leader understands that change can be harnessed for the organization's benefit through small evolutionary steps that allow it to continually improve and adapt. These leaders know that they will always have to face change, so they take incremental steps to help the organization always be prepared to successfully adapt. They understand that as change continues, the evolution of their organization also shifts. Therefore, taking small, effortless steps, rather than waiting and taking broad, overwhelming actions to catch up with change, is much less painful and frightening. This process allays employees' personal fears and seamlessly integrates an endless series of evolutionary steps into the operational workplace environment.

## POINTS TO PONDER — SOMETHING TO THINK ABOUT

1. While no one likes change, do you fear or embrace it?
2. Do you feel personally threatened by the changes in your industry and organization?

## TRAINING ACTIVITY — APPLICATION & ACTION PLAN

1. Determine the biggest challenges and changes in your organization.
2. Identify how your organization must adapt to embrace these changes.
3. Ascertain the opportunities that these changes will offer your company.
4. Pinpoint small, effortless steps that your organization can take to evolve in the face of change.

# 4

# Recognizing When Change Is Occurring

Whether managers and leaders wish to admit it, they have already been impacted by change. Change is continuous; therefore, it is important for leaders to know how to recognize when change is affecting or about to affect their organization. This knowledge allows them to be proactive rather than reactive.

## IMPLICATIONS – WHAT THIS MEANS TO YOU

The force and impact of change experienced at the end of the 20th century and into the beginning of the 21st was on a scale so enormous that it had never been experienced before. The closest comparison is with the advent of the Industrial Age in the 1840s, when many industrial giants rose up and created the working model that most companies built themselves on.

It is important for leaders to understand that the current pace, dynamics and scope of change is unparalleled in human history. The industrial model that once worked so well is effectively gone. Some companies continue to cling to the old model, but they will be either forced to change or eliminated as viable organizations. Just like the Industrial Revolution sparked opportunity, so do the forces of change today. The leader who can recognize the opportunities will find new products, services, career opportunities and growth at their fingertips.

Nobody likes to change. As stated in previous lessons, change threatens individual and organizational comfort zones. But it is impossible to hold back the forces of change; the organization that tries will ultimately fail.

While the forces of change have already swept over most, if not all, organizations, there are factors that individual leaders should be aware of to help them recognize the pressures that change brings to their organization.

## The Rules Have Changed

One of the most disquieting elements of change for individuals is that the rules of the game—which are needed to succeed and advance in a career—have been altered and continue to alter. The time of working hard and slowly advancing in the organization is gone. Many workers that entered the workforce in the 1950s, 1960s and 1970s are familiar with this model. However, during their personal journey of advancement, they awoke to find a younger force of managers taking over business in the 1990s during the dot-com boom. Hard work and success were no longer as relevant as ambitious goals and plans. The dot-com bust was followed by a rapid economic downturn. And once again the rules have changed. Undoubtedly, they will continue to change in response to the market and economy.

The current climate has a need for managers, leaders and workers who are flexible in the face of compelling change and willing to adapt and evolve as needed. Flexibility allows organizations to adapt and use the momentum to their advantage.

## The Need for Speed

The impact of technology continues to breed and foster changes that are increasingly buttressed by an interconnected world. Email, phone, fax and the Internet connect most employees globally. Consequently, a flow of information that once might have taken months or even years, now takes only days or minutes to seamlessly move from one end of the world to the other. The rapid flow of information increases competition and decreases planning and implementation cycles. The time available for a company to plan and rollout a new product or production facility continues to get shorter; windows of opportunity are becoming miniscule. This is not to say they don't exist anymore, but a five-year planning cycle that existed a decade ago has probably shrunk to one-and-a-half years at best.

### Decreased Stability

Managers, leaders and employees all sense that the stability that once existed within their organization is decreasing. Companies are forced to adapt to these changes or face their demise as a viable entity. As companies come to grips with this reality, structural changes occur within the organization: layers of management are eliminated and workforces are downsized. To many employees, what was once a stable working environment appears to have slipped into a chaotic mess, increasing their personal fears about the future.

### Results Diminish

When production and operational models that worked so well in the past are no longer effective, it indicates that change is occurring within the organization. The shift is evident in the overall decrease in outcomes and results. As an increasingly sophisticated customer base demands higher quality products and as the competition becomes more innovative, a company not on board with change will often see their own production and efficiency diminish while their customers complain and demand more from them.

While these factors may appear detrimental, they are signals that give leaders the opportunity to adapt instead of fail in the marketplace.

### Increased Frustration and Resistance

All of the circumstances described in this lesson can increase the frustrations of managers, leaders and employees as they deal with the pressures that change brings to the organization and come to terms with their ability to adapt to it. When individuals are inflexible and feel comfortable in their current position, they will resist change in an attempt to defend their position and power base.

The organization can find itself caught in a perpetual cycle of instability fueled by its people's frustration with and resistance to change. For the organization to escape this cycle, individuals must either eliminate these barriers to change or learn to reluctantly accept them and adapt to the changes forced upon them.

## Shift to Niche Markets

Some organizations have been able to successfully service large and varied markets with their products or services. As competitive pressures increase, however, many of these companies must rethink their production and output strategies in order to cater to more tightly focused and carefully targeted niche markets. This trend will increase until ultimately a shift occurs where technology allows companies to completely customize their products and services and leave traditional mass production behind.

## Increased Globalization

It was once comforting to work in a production facility located in a small community in the Midwest or South. It was as if these facilities were isolated from the rest of the country; they were allowed to move at their own slower pace. However, technology and globalization have brought the same forces of change that first appeared in the larger metropolitan areas to even the most isolated plants and facilities. Now these facilities are connected through multinational companies and conglomerates and are often forced to move and to compete with competitors in Asia, Europe and the Pacific Rim.

### POINTS TO PONDER – SOMETHING TO THINK ABOUT

1. When dealing with organizational change in the past, have you been reactive or proactive?
2. Did you fear any changes? If so, did those fears materialize?

## TRAINING ACTIVITY – APPLICATION & ACTION PLAN

1. Identify major changes you have observed in your organization.
2. Using hindsight, determine if there were signs of these changes before they struck.
3. Pinpoint possible signs of current and future changes.
4. Focus on ways that you can take advantage of the opportunities that these changes bring.

# 5

# Coming to Grips with the Ramifications of Change

The global competitive forces that are bearing down on all organizations have altered the nature of change in the workplace. Whereas at one time companies could deal with large and monumental changes as a singular event, now these forces require them to continually adapt. Change should be seen as part of an organization's everyday operation rather than as a mere anomaly.

## IMPLICATIONS – WHAT THIS MEANS TO YOU

The concept of "change management" was introduced not too long ago as a way for organizations to minimize the damage that change brings to the workplace while simultaneously strengthening the healing process. Its use has reassured employees that adapting will offer their company a better future by providing them with the means of surviving change. Change management creates a sense of urgency within the organization that has compelled many employees to grudgingly accept changes.

Leaders must understand, however, that no organization can survive a nonstop series of supposed emergencies associated with change and still hope to successfully adapt. One "emergency" after another serves to desensitize employees, so that when an actual emergency does occur, the organization will fail to adequately react to it. Additionally, continual emergencies will only burnout the managers, leaders and employees responding to them. The reality is that perpetual change is here to stay, and leaders must learn to embrace it and use it to their advantage. This means redefining what change means to the organization as well as clarifying the risks associated with it.

## STRATEGIES, TIPS & TECHNIQUES TO APPLY

The most recent model many organizations utilized to deal with change began as a response to internal stagnation. Stagnation often caused discomfort that prompted senior executives to make a decision to adjust. As a result, these organizations started to prepare for change, hoping to adequately adapt in order to survive the conflicts, clashes and failures associated with upheaval. Organizations that survived would either walk away or see the change through to some sort of beneficial fruition. Today, as changes happen more quickly and frequently, adapting to change is more difficult and expensive.

As smart leaders understand the increasing velocity and dynamics of change, they are learning to embrace the idea of an always-shifting organization, where change is no longer considered a threat but simply part of the job. This attitude change in leadership produces several positive outcomes for organizations, as outlined below.

### New Ways of Thinking

New ideas and concepts are often not warmly accepted in most companies because they can challenge existing strategies that probably helped make the organization successful. Rather than be far-sighted and see how strategies will necessarily be different in the future, many decision makers in an organization are myopic, threatened by future changes and associated ramifications. Leaders who attempt to shake up the status quo often fear personal criticism and attacks, and are therefore intimidated into silence.

As people embrace the concept of an always-changing organization, new ways of thinking become part of the way the business grows, evolves and adapts to change. New ideas are thus welcomed and examined. Through brainstorming, ideas are expanded as individuals build on each concept until new organizational models are developed, tested and ultimately implemented.

### New Ideas and Concepts

As new ways of thinking are developed, new ideas and concepts evolve. Rather than dismiss them outright, organizations and leaders are more willing to test the ideas to see if they are valid. Even when the tests fail, leaders dissect them and learn from mistakes. Through a series of tests, more new ideas are encouraged. Innovation is welcome, and the organization slowly adapts to continual change by evolving with the implementation of new ideas and concepts that have been thoroughly tested. It is a slow, incremental process, but it is also less stressful on the organization because one idea after another is implemented.

### New Opportunities

Throughout the process of introducing and testing new ideas and concepts, leaders will be able to identify new opportunities for the organization to take advantage of. Some will be minor, while others will provide exceptional opportunities for growth; however, all will give the organization the means of adapting to change, increasing efficiency and productivity, and potentially increasing overall market share and dominance.

### Evolution in Response to Change

The greatest opportunity an organization can seize is a gradual evolution in response to change (as opposed to large, expensive, last minute responses when pressed to survive). Just as plants and animals evolve and adapt to their environment, organizations must learn to do the same. Incremental change doesn't produce personal fear and stress, and is not threatening to the organization's survival. Gradual adaptation helps buffer the company from the conflicts, clashes and failures often associated with change. While pilots and tests of new ideas and concepts may fail, they won't produce a backlash within the organization; instead, they will be considered a natural part of the company's growth, change and eventual evolution.

## POINTS TO PONDER — SOMETHING TO THINK ABOUT

1. Do you see how change is continuous in your organization?
2. Can you accept the concept of an always-changing organization? Why or why not?

## TRAINING ACTIVITY — APPLICATION & ACTION PLAN

Consider the area you supervise, and begin to look for new ideas and concepts to test that, if successful, will help the organization take small, incremental steps in the face of continual change.

1. Define the idea and concept.
2. Run a small-scale test or pilot that can assess the validity of the idea.
3. Analyze the results and identify the lessons learned, whether a success or failure.
4. Modify and test again until the idea is refined.
5. Introduce the validated idea under your supervision.

# 6

# Managing Change

The management of change can be personally frightening for many leaders. They fear criticism and personal attacks from associates and superiors. Most importantly, they dread the potential failure associated with change and the possible impact of such failure on their career.

## IMPLICATIONS – WHAT THIS MEANS TO YOU

Most organizations make it easier to say "no" to a project that is associated with change than to approve one. When they reject a project, managers protect themselves from having to justify tough decisions and facing the criticism that comes with a failing project. Moreover, when approving a project, many managers discover they are forced to work harder, take more risks and suffer more criticism than they are prepared to deal with. And if they do fail, they often discover that the less innovative and more risk-averse associates are rewarded by the organization.

This is important for leaders to understand because if the above scenario is a reality in their organization, it places a damper on their ability to innovate in the face of change. However, innovative leaders can take solace in the fact that much of the undue criticism heaped upon them is often based on misdirected frustrations; in fact, individuals are often unhappy with what is already happening in their organization, but have a hard time grasping the need to evolve to maintain or renew success. Leaders must come up with ways to overcome this internal inertia as part of their responsibility to manage change in their organization.

## STRATEGIES, TIPS & TECHNIQUES TO APPLY

Organizations can and will change—it is a matter of choice. Leaders faced with the responsibility of managing change in their organization must overcome the specific challenges described below if they want to be successful.

### Fear of Failure

Fear on all levels is the biggest challenge for leaders. There may be several ways for leaders to use early successes and ideas that can be tested and refined, and then leverage them into more substantial achievements. However, they are often faced with senior management's fear of failure and their own fear of being criticized by investors, customers and even the competition. Often leaders can hesitate to enact change simply because it might affect just a few customers, even if that same change can increase the satisfaction of the majority of their clients.

### Dealing with Committees

Leaders should understand that committees in most organizations are one of the primary barriers to change. While small committees can be effective, large groups can be impossible to deal with. If fact, most organizations make it easy for a single committee member to say "no" and veto a new idea or concept—thus requiring a unanimous "yes" for anything to move forward. Consequently, the larger the committee, the longer it will take a leader to convince each member that a new concept or idea is worthwhile.

### Handling Critics

For most critics, adopting a new idea, concept or strategy means turning away from the focus that is currently making the organization successful. Most of these critics see change not as an evolution of ideas and concepts that makes the organization better, faster and more competitive, but as a zero-sum game where one side wins at the expense of the other. The arguments they espouse are often formed by their personal fear of failure.

Leaders can effectually deal with such critics by setting ground rules for criticism, including:

1. Criticize an idea based on how well it meets its objectives. If the critics don't care for the objectives, then the objectives must be discussed as a separate matter.
2. Weigh the idea against the status quo, being sure to look at present failures and problems.
3. If a critic doesn't like an idea, he or she must come up with an alternative. A lack of a solution is not an acceptable solution.
4. Criticism for criticism's sake should not be tolerated, nor should personal attacks.

## Redefine Change and Failure

One of the biggest aspects of managing change is in redefining the rules. What was acceptable in the past may not be acceptable in the current climate of change. Therefore, leaders must redefine failure as it pertains to the organization. The fear of failure results in inertia as organizations struggle to maintain the status quo. And, ironically, maintaining the status quo in the face of change will always result in failure. As previously stated, a lack of a solution is not an acceptable solution.

Additionally, leaders must redefine change within the organization. They must make it clear that continuous change is the normal state of affairs. Accordingly, it must be redefined as something that is an expected part of every normal job, not something that is a cause for panic and anxiety. If individuals accept this reformulation, then risk will automatically be redefined; when change is a normal part one's job, the risks associated with change are thus minimized. This shift in perspective helps reduce personal levels of stress and anxiety and makes the responsibility of managing change easier as leaders help their organization evolve through small, incremental steps.

## POINTS TO PONDER — SOMETHING TO THINK ABOUT

1. What do you see as your biggest challenge as you manage change?
2. How do you see the status quo in your organization being protected from change?

## TRAINING ACTIVITY — APPLICATION & ACTION PLAN

1. Determine what defines the status quo in your organization.
2. Examine how the status quo hinders the need to change.
3. Analyze the best ways to challenge the status quo.
4. Identify the incremental steps you can take to move the organization forward.

# 7

# Strategies to Personally Manage Change

The Greek word *metamórphosis* means, "changed or transformed." When individuals accept that change is a natural part of their organizational environment, they cease resisting it and are thus transformed. They henceforth evolve with the ongoing changes that take place in the organization.

## IMPLICATIONS – WHAT THIS MEANS TO YOU

Most people fear change. In the workplace, leaders' fears are fed by a feeling that if they attempt to initiate change, they will lose their job because their superiors will not support their efforts. Leaders also resist change due to the time constraints associated with their existing responsibilities. If time is taken from these, they fear their core business will fail, resulting in everyone being out of a job. Additionally, change is an unknown. Since leaders might fear what the unknown will bring to their organization, they attempt to ignore it, hoping it just goes away.

Leaders must comprehend that what they fear is the organization-threatening choices that companies are faced with after ignoring the earlier and obvious need for change. At such a point, the organization has no other option but to make a decision or perish. Leaders must learn to accept that change is here to stay and something that they must deal with in small and incremental steps that allow the organization to evolve. Taking the proper far-sighted approach ensures that a company will not have to face the organization-threatening changes that everyone fears.

## STRATEGIES, TIPS & TECHNIQUES TO APPLY

Before leaders can deal with organizational change they must first accept change personally and professionally. If they can hone personal techniques to handle and adapt to change, then they can adjust these techniques to the workplace and their leadership style. These methods are discussed below:

### Acceptance

Individuals must learn to accept change. Whether they realize it or not, most people currently in the workplace grew up in a dynamic environment characterized by change. Since the 1960s, society has been subject to drastic change stemming from events such as the civil rights movement, Vietnam and Watergate. All of these pivotal events spurred waves of change that have impacted everyone's lives to this day.

Since the 1980s, society has seen monumental advances in technology that have changed everyone's lives as well. The introduction of the personal computer, fax machines, cell phones, email, VCRs, the Internet, mobile computing devices and a host of other technological devices have literally changed the face of business and personal lives.

Whether or not one would admit it, life has changed, and most changes have been quietly accepted and integrated into many people's lives. And many would agree that it has made their lives easier and better. So if people fear change, then they would be well served to go back over their lives to see how they have handled and adapted to change. Most would probably agree that it has been a slow, incremental process that they have hardly noticed, except in hindsight.

### Observe Change

Every time individuals buy a new car, a new electronic device such as a computer or DVD player, or a new consumer product such as self-rising pizza crust, they are accepting change. Since these changes are small, they are not the life-threatening events everyone fears; yet, they are still changes. Obviously, individuals can resist or deny change by choosing not to purchase these products, but most feel they have no other option, and subsequently think nothing of it.

As leaders learn to handle change in the workplace, they should begin by observing the countless changes made in their personal lives. They should note the impact these have made and how they felt about the results. These reflections should help leaders learn how to adapt in a constantly changing workplace environment.

## Learn Personal Flexibility

Inflexible individuals have the most difficulty adapting to change. These are often older people who grew up in a more stable pre-1960s environment. They liked the way things were and resisted even the smallest changes. However, this description does not characterize everyone who grew up during this period. Many, in fact, have found the changes in society and technology liberating, making their lives easier and more productive.

It is not age so much as mindset that is important. Leaders must learn to become personally flexible. Anyone can become more flexible by learning to change some of the minor details in their lives, such as eating at a new restaurant, rearranging the furniture in their homes and offices, changing a hair style or taking a vacation somewhere new or unknown.

When individuals learn to be personally flexible and adaptable, they can easily do the same in the workplace. It starts with taking small, incremental steps and then observing the effects and consequences.

## Look for Small Opportunities

Life outside the workplace provides individuals with many opportunities to change and improve their lives. Individuals should become more aware of the countless opportunities for change. Most people can make these changes without a second thought. As a personal lesson in accepting change, leaders should look for small opportunities they can seize to change their lives. They should learn to evaluate their personal decisions and analyze the impact these small changes have on their lives.

### Experiment

Individuals should experiment with various methods of change. When they experiment, observe and learn from the results in their personal lives, it should be easy to translate these lessons to the workplace.

It is notable that most people are more conservative about changes in their personal lives than at work because they have to pay for the changes out of their own pocket. At work, on the other hand, they are spending the company's money. This is not to say they have lost their thrift altogether, but it makes a difference that the monetary costs associated with change are not their direct burden.

## POINTS TO PONDER — SOMETHING TO THINK ABOUT

1. How aware are you of the changes that constantly occur in your life?
2. If you accept constant change in your personal life, why are you afraid of workplace change?

## TRAINING ACTIVITY — APPLICATION & ACTION PLAN

Observe the impact of change on your life.

1. Think about an earlier time in your life (go back two or three decades, if possible), and describe the home you owned or rented, the car you drove and the conveniences you used, such as a computer, VCR or phone.
2. Describe your life today in the same manner.
3. Compare then to now and note the changes that have occurred.

# 8

# Preventing Personal Burnout

Many leaders will associate the implementation of change in their organization with elevated levels of stress, frustration and anxiety. These pressures, combined with a typical staff reduction that often requires leaders to accomplish more with less, can lead to personal burnout.

## IMPLICATIONS — WHAT THIS MEANS TO YOU

Change management, as incorporated in many organizational plans and strategies, often leads to personal burnout, as rather than take small, incremental steps that allow organizations to evolve, many will stagnate and resist change until the company is severely threatened and must make huge, destabilizing adjustments to survive.

It is important for leaders to understand that large, overwhelming changes will typically shake up the entire organization as wholesale modifications occur in the way business is conducted. The process is time intensive and traumatic for everyone involved. People require time to recuperate after the event is over; wholesale changes often result in personal burnout.

## STRATEGIES, TIPS & TECHNIQUES TO APPLY

Undoubtedly, quick and/or frequent change can lead to burnout.

However, even in the face of ongoing change, leaders can use the strategies outlined in this section to defend against burnout and frustration.

## Part of the Job

Effective leaders accept that change is a normal function associated with their jobs. In this way, change is no longer perceived as an event that threatens the organization, but simply a normal function of everyday business activity. Leaders who embrace change plan small, incremental adjustments that help their organization slowly evolve and adapt. As a result, the company will eventually see an increase in productivity and efficiency. All it takes is a change in the leader's perception to reduce the stress and pressures that he or she once associated with organizational change.

## Anticipate Rather Than Resist

When people oppose change in their organization, they end up focusing their energy on resistance rather than acceptance. This focus saps the energy required to maintain productivity and effectiveness, which ultimately leads to burnout.

On the other hand, leaders who accept and anticipate change learn to harness its momentum to their benefit and use that energy to enact change throughout the organization, producing positive outcomes and results.

## Pace

When organizations implement wholesale changes out of necessity, it can be overwhelming. Many of these changes include layoffs, which increase the intensity of the situation and overburden the leader. In turn, stress and anxiety levels go up, resulting in personal burnout.

However, when leaders plan for ongoing change, adjustments are made in small, incremental steps that allow the organization to transform itself on its own terms. Once done, wholesale organizational change is eliminated, as is the stress and intensity of change.

### Incorporate

The incorporation of small, incremental changes into daily activities allows the organization to grow and evolve while simultaneously increasing productivity, effectiveness and efficiency. The incremental nature of change allows leaders to build it seamlessly into the organizational culture. When the organization accepts change as a daily occurrence, leaders don't really feel pressured nor do they experience high levels of personal stress and anxiety. This greatly reduces personal burnout.

### Experiment

Leaders that learn to accept and incorporate change into their daily responsibilities also learn the value of experimenting with new ideas and concepts. They discover that small changes can be tested with minimal impact and that lessons can be learned from all successes and failures. These lessons are ultimately incorporated into adaptations made by the organization. Experimentation also helps leaders reduce risks associated with change. And less risk equals less stress, frustration and anxiety—all of which are associated with burnout.

#### POINTS TO PONDER – SOMETHING TO THINK ABOUT

1. How stressful has change been on you?
2. What do you feel contributed to your elevated levels of stress, frustration and anxiety?

## TRAINING ACTIVITY – APPLICATION & ACTION PLAN

Every organization has experienced wholesale changes over the past decade.

1. Recall the last major change your organization underwent and the stresses it placed on you.

2. When you have implemented small, incremental changes, what kind of stress did you experience?
3. Compare and contrast the two, including the results, effects and associated stress levels.
4. Identify which is more effective and easier to manage.

# About the Author

Timothy F. Bednarz, Ph.D. is CEO of the American Management Development Group, Inc. For over 20 years he has researched, designed and authored hundreds of learning and development programs used by Fortune 1000 companies.

He is also the author of *Great! What Makes Leaders Great. What They Did, How They Did It and What You Can Learn from It* (2011).

## Speaking Availability

Timothy F. Bednarz, Ph.D. is available for speaking engagements for your next meeting or association event. He can be contacted at 800-654-4935 or by e-mail at timothy.bednarz@majorium.com.

## Bulk Sales

Bulk sales of this book or any other titles available from Majorium Business Press. Inquiries can be directed to sales@majorium.com, or by phone at 800-6654-4935.

# Quick Order Form

**Fax orders:** 715-342-1118. Send this form.

**Telephone orders:** Call 800-654-4935 toll-free. Have your credit card ready.

**Email orders:** sales@majorium.com

**Postal orders:** Majorium Business Press, 2025 Main Street, Stevens Point, WI 54481, USA.

**Please send the following books:**

______________________________________________________________

______________________________________________________________

______________________________________________________________

______________________________________________________________

**Please send more FREE information on:**

❑Catalog ❑Speaking/Seminars ❑Mailing Lists ❑Consulting

Name: ________________________________________________________

Address: ______________________________________________________

City: ______________________________ State: _____ Zip: __________

Telephone: ____________________________________________________

Email address: _________________________________________________

**Sales tax:** Please add 5.5% for products shipped to Wisconsin addresses.

**Shipping by air:**

**United States:** $4.00 for first book and $2.00 for each additional product.

**International:** $9.00 for first book; $5.00 for each additional product (estimate).